Learning to Read, Step by Step!

Ready to Read **Preschool–Kindergarten**
• big type and easy words • rhyme and rhythm • picture clues
For children who know the alphabet and are eager to
begin reading.

Reading with Help **Preschool–Grade 1**
• basic vocabulary • short sentences • simple stories
For children who recognize familiar words and sound out
new words with help.

Reading on Your Own **Grades 1–3**
• engaging characters • easy-to-follow plots • popular topics
For children who are ready to read on their own.

Reading Paragraphs **Grades 2–3**
• challenging vocabulary • short paragraphs • exciting stories
For newly independent readers who read simple sentences
with confidence.

Ready for Chapters **Grades 2–4**
• chapters • longer paragraphs • full-color art
For children who want to take the plunge into chapter books
but still like colorful pictures.

STEP INTO READING® is designed to give every child a successful
reading experience. The grade levels are only guides; children will progress
through the steps at their own speed, developing confidence in their reading.
The F&P Text Level on the back cover serves as another tool to help you
choose the right book for your child.

Remember, a lifetime love of reading starts with a single step!

For David—slow, but steady! —B.B.

Text copyright © 2016 by Bonnie Bader

Photograph credits: cover: baby sloth © Thinkstock/Snic320, climbing sloth © Thinkstock/ Eric Isselée; pages 3, 15: © Getty Images/Hoberman Collection; page 4: © Thinkstock/ JonathanNicholls; page 5: © Thinkstock/SivelstreSelva; pages 1, 6–7: © Thinkstock/Eric Isselée; page 8: © Thinkstock/ctrlaplus1; page 9: © Thinkstock/miroslav_1; page 10: © Thinkstock/Julio Viard; page 11: © Thinkstock/JackF; page 12: © Thinkstock/Eric Isselée; page 13: © Thinkstock/ webguzs; page 14: © Thinkstock/JackKa; page 16: © Thinkstock/Jozev; page 17: © Getty Images/ Wolfgang Kaehler; page 18: © Getty Images/Hoberman Collection; page 19: © Corbis; page 20: © Thinkstock/Eric Middelkoop; page 21: © Getty Images/DEA/C. DANI I. JESKE; pages 22–23: © Thinkstock/Seubsai; page 24: ants © Thinkstock/onlyyouqj, grasshopper © Thinkstock/ Andreas Argirakis, lizard © Thinkstock/ananaline, mosquito © Thinkstock/JoyTasa; page 25: © Corbis/Suzi Eszterhas; page 26: © Getty Images/RODRIGO ARANGUA; page 27: © Corbis/Piotr Naskrecki; page 28: © Corbis/James Christensen; page 29: © Corbis/Wayne Lynch; page 30: © Getty Images/RODRIGO ARANGUA; page 31: © Thinkstock/Adam_C_King; page 32: © Thinkstock/tane-mahuta.

Visit us on the Web!
StepIntoReading.com
rhcbooks.com

Educators and librarians, for a variety of teaching tools, visit us at
RHTeachersLibrarians.com

Library of Congress Cataloging-in-Publication Data is available upon request.
ISBN 978-0-593-43244-0 (trade) — ISBN 978-0-593-43245-7 (lib. bdg.)

Printed in the United States of America
10 9 8 7 6 5 4 3 2 1

This book has been officially leveled by using the F&P Text Level Gradient™ Leveling System.

SLOW, SLOW SLOTHS

by Bonnie Bader

Random House 🏠 New York

Slow,

slow

sloths!

6

Central America

Rain forests

South America

Sloths are mammals.
They live in the
rain forests of Central
and South America.

Sloths have long arms
and long fur.
Are they in the
same family
as monkeys?

No!

Sloths are in the same family

as armadillos.

And anteaters.

There are two types of sloths.

The two-toed sloth has two claws

on its front feet.

The three-toed sloth
has three claws on its
front feet.

All sloths have round heads.

And three- to four-inch claws.

And little ears.

And short tails.

And sad-looking eyes.

But the three-toed sloth

looks like it is always smiling!

Sloths are born high up

in the trees.

Baby sloths cling to

their mothers' bellies

until they can take care

of themselves.

A young sloth likes to stay close

to its mother.

It can live with her

for up to four years.

Now it is all grown up.

It is about two feet long.

It weighs between 8 and 17

pounds.

Sloths like to live
by themselves.

They sleep a lot.

Sloths sleep between

15 and 20 hours a day.

Two-toed sloths

are awake at night.

Sloths hook their claws onto

tree branches.

They hang upside down

by their long arms.

Sloths sleep and sleep and sleep.

Sloths don't eat much.

They sometimes eat small insects.

Or small lizards.

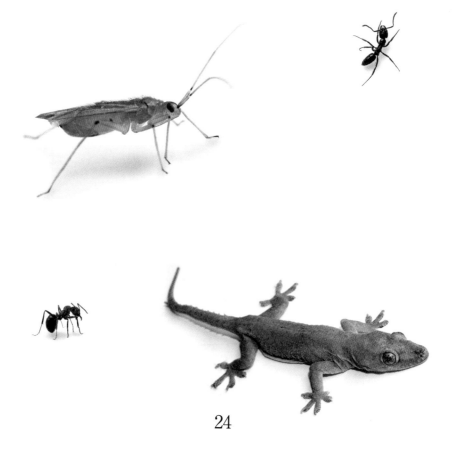

But they mostly eat leaves.

Leaves do not give them

much energy.

This is one reason sloths are

so slow!

The sloth's long claws make it hard to walk on the ground. So it stays in the trees.

Some sloths stay in the same tree

for years.

The only time they come down

is to go to the bathroom.

Or to go for a swim.

Plop! The sloth falls from the tree
into the river.

Sloths are great swimmers.

Sloths move so slowly that algae
(say: AL-gee) grows on their fur.
This green plant helps sloths hide
from their enemies.

But they can't always hide.

Here comes a harpy eagle!

Swipe! The sloth bats at

the harpy eagle with

its long, sharp claws.

The sloth hisses.

It lets out a loud yell.

The harpy eagle flies away.

The sloth is tired

from fighting off its enemy.

It slowly climbs up the tree

and goes to sleep.

Sleep tight, slow, slow sloth!